WEIGHT LOSS SURGERY FRIENDLY

# Single Serves

## JUSTINE HAWKE

ACCREDITED PRACTISING DIETITIAN | ACCREDITED NUTRITIONIST

# Contents

**Meatballs & Patties**  5

Beef with Feta & Prunes  7
Bocconcini Filled Mediterranean  7
Mexican Chicken  9
Thai Inspired Chicken  9
Beef & Dukkah  11
Greek Style Lamb  11

**Muffin Tins**  13

*Rice Muffins*
Chargrilled Pepper & Tomato  15
Roasted Pumpkin, Pine Nut & Spinach  15
Chicken, Bacon & Thyme  17

*Egg Muffins*
Sweet Potato, Zucchini & Feta  17
Bacon, Mushroom & Tomato  19
Smoked Salmon, Cream Cheese & Dill  19

*Mini Meatloaves*
Chicken, Pesto & Pine Nut  21
Italian Style  21
Turkey & Cranberry  23
Pork, Apple & Pistachio  23

Enchilada Cups  25
Lasagne Muffins  25

**Ramekins**  27

Mini Shepherd's Pie  29
Basic Meat Sauce  29
Mini Mexican Chicken Bowls  31
Chicken Curry with Pappadums  31
Salmon Mornay  33
Chicken, Leek & Mushroom Pies  33

# Meatballs & Patties

..............................

*Meatballs and patties are great to make ahead of time and keep on hand in the fridge or freezer. You can easily serve a couple with fresh salad for lunch, or use them to form the base of your dinner. Portable and protein packed, how could you go wrong?*

*Most recipes in this section can be made into patties or balls. Each ball uses approximately one eighth of a cup of mince mixture, and patties use approximately one quarter of a cup of mince mixture, making it easier to control your portions.*

## Beef with Feta & Prunes

MAKES 20 SMALL MEATBALLS
MAKES 10 SMALL PATTIES

500g lean beef mince
¾ cup rolled oats
40g feta, crumbled
8 prunes, finely diced
2 tablespoons fruit chutney
1 egg

Place all ingredients in a bowl and mix well. Roll into walnut sized balls or small patties. Place onto a non-stick or oiled oven tray and place in a preheated oven at 180°C for 15 minutes or until cooked through and golden.

Suitable to freeze.

Nutrition information (per 2 meatballs or 1 patty): kilojoules 640, calories 152, protein 15.5g, fat 6g, saturated fat 2.5g, carbohydrate 8g, fibre 1g.

If you are using our Nutrition for Weight Loss Surgery Meal Plans, one serve of this recipe provides the following number of serves from each of the following food groups:
1/2 GRAINS
1 PROTEIN
1 FATS

## Bocconcini Filled Mediterranean

MAKES 20 SMALL MEATBALLS
NOT SUITABLE FOR PATTIES

500g lean beef mince
1 cup multigrain breadcrumbs
6 cherry tomatoes, finely diced
40g chargrilled red capsicum, finely diced
2 tablespoons basil, chopped
2 tablespoons tomato relish
1 egg
Salt and pepper to taste
5 mini bocconcini balls, cut into quarters

Place all ingredients (except bocconcini) in a bowl and mix well. Roll into walnut sized balls. Make a small hole and press in bocconcini, then encase within the meat mixture. Place onto a non-stick or oiled oven tray and place in a pre-heated oven at 180°C for 15 minutes or until cooked through and golden.

Suitable to freeze.

Nutrition information (per 2 meatballs): kilojoules 725, calories 172, protein 17g, fat 6.5g, saturated fat 3g, carbohydrate 10.5g, fibre 1g.

If you are using our Nutrition for Weight Loss Surgery Meal Plans, one serve of this recipe provides the following number of serves from each of the following food groups:
1 GRAINS
1 PROTEIN
1 FATS

# Thai Inspired Chicken

MAKES 20 SMALL MEATBALLS
MAKES 10 SMALL PATTIES

500g chicken breast mince
1 teaspoon red curry paste (or to taste)
1/3 cup sweet chili sauce
1 egg
1/3 cup low fat cottage cheese
¾ cup multigrain breadcrumbs
1 tablespoon reduced salt soy sauce
¼ cup coriander leaves, roughly chopped
Drizzle of olive oil for cooking

Place all ingredients in a bowl and mix well. Roll into walnut sized balls or small patties. Place onto a non-stick or oiled oven tray and place in a preheated oven at 180°C for 15 minutes or until cooked through and golden.

Note: The mixture is quite wet. Use baking paper or a silicone mat on a cooking tray to prevent the meatballs sticking.

Suitable to freeze.

Nutrition information (per 2 meatballs or 1 patty): kilojoules 590, calories 140, protein 12.5g, fat 5.5g, saturated fat 1.5g, carbohydrate 10g, fibre 0.5g.

If you are using our Nutrition for Weight Loss Surgery Meal Plans, one serve of this recipe provides the following number of serves from each of the following food groups:
1/2 GRAINS
1/2 PROTEIN
1 FATS

# Mexican Chicken

MAKES 20 SMALL MEATBALLS
MAKES 10 SMALL PATTIES

500g lean chicken mince
1 small red onion, grated
35g sachet salt reduced taco seasoning
1 cup multigrain breadcrumbs
1 egg
Salsa for serving

Place all ingredients (except salsa) in a bowl and mix well. Roll into walnut sized balls or small patties. Place onto a non-stick or oiled oven tray. Place in a pre-heated oven at 180°C for 15 minutes or until cooked through and golden. Serve with salsa.

Suitable to freeze.

Note: These meatballs are delicious served in a pita pocket with shredded lettuce and fresh tomato, but can just as easily be enjoyed with salsa on their own.

Nutrition information (per 2 meatballs or 1 patty, without salsa): kilojoules 570, calories 136, protein 12g, fat 5g, saturated fat 1.5g, carbohydrate 10g, fibre 1g.

If you are using our Nutrition for Weight Loss Surgery Meal Plans, one serve of this recipe provides the following number of serves from each of the following food groups:
1/2 GRAINS
1/2 PROTEIN
1 FATS

# Greek Style Lamb

MAKES 20 SMALL MEATBALLS
MAKES 10 SMALL PATTIES

500g lean lamb mince
1 cup multigrain breadcrumbs
¼ cup Parmesan cheese, finely grated
2 teaspoons dried oregano
Juice of half a lemon
1 clove garlic, crushed
60g feta, crumbled
2 eggs
Tzatziki to serve

Combine all ingredients (except tzatziki) in a bowl and mix well. Roll into walnut sized balls or small patties. Place onto a non-stick or oiled oven tray and place in a pre-heated oven at 180°C for 15 minutes or until cooked through and golden. Serve with tzatziki.

Suitable to freeze.

Nutrition information (per two meatballs or one patty): kilojoules 785, calories 187, protein 15g, fat 10g, saturated fat 4.5g, carbohydrate 8.5g, fibre 0.5g.

If you are using our Nutrition for Weight Loss Surgery Meal Plans, one serve of this recipe provides the following number of serves from each of the following food groups:
1/2 GRAINS
1/2 PROTEIN
2 FATS

# Beef & Dukkah

MAKES 20 SMALL MEATBALLS
MAKES 10 SMALL PATTIES

500g lean beef mince
Juice of half a lemon
1 teaspoon lemon zest
½ cup multigrain breadcrumbs
2 tablespoons spicy fruit chutney
1 egg
1/3 cup dukkah

Place all ingredients (except dukkah) in a bowl and mix well. Roll into walnut sized balls or small patties. Roll lightly in dukkah. Place onto a non-stick or oiled oven tray and place in a pre-heated oven at 180°C for 15 minutes or until cooked through and golden.

Suitable to freeze.

Note: These meatballs are delicious served with hommus and tabouli.

Nutrition information (per two meatballs or one patty): kilojoules 605, calories 143, protein 15g, fat 6.5g, saturated fat 2g, carbohydrate 6g.

If you are using our Nutrition for Weight Loss Surgery Meal Plans, one serve of this recipe provides the following number of serves from each of the following food groups:
1/2 GRAINS
1/2 PROTEIN
1 FATS

# Muffin Tins

...............................

*Who would have picked the humble muffin tin as the ultimate portion control tool in your kitchen? At half a cup per serve, you can confidently enjoy 1-2 of these delights for lunch (or dinner). Make plenty and stock your freezer so it is always easy to make the healthy choice.*

*To ensure your delicious creations don't stick, invest in silicone muffin trays, or line your trays with baking paper if you prefer.*

# Chargrilled Pepper & Tomato Rice Muffins

MAKES 8 MUFFINS

1 red onion, finely diced

2/3 cup raw brown rice, prepared according to directions on packet

1 cup grated cheese

3 eggs, whisked

2 medium tomatoes, diced

50g chargrilled red peppers, diced

Sauté red onion until cooked through. Add prepared rice, cheese and eggs and combine. Add tomato and peppers. Spoon mixture into muffin trays and bake in a pre-heated oven at 180°C for 15 - 20 minutes, or until cooked through and golden.

Suitable to freeze.

Nutrition information (per muffin): kilojoules 930, calories 221, protein 12g, fat 12.5g, saturated fat 8g, carbohydrate 14.5g, fibre 1.5g.

If you are using our Nutrition for Weight Loss Surgery Meal Plans, one serve of this recipe provides the following number of serves from each of the following food groups:

1 GRAINS

1/2 PROTEIN

2 1/2 FATS

# Roasted Pumpkin, Pine Nut & Spinach Rice Muffins

MAKES 8 MUFFINS

1 red onion, finely diced

2/3 cup raw brown rice, prepared according to directions on packet

1 cup grated cheese

3 eggs, whisked

150g pumpkin, peeled, cut into small cubes and roasted

30g pine nuts

40g baby spinach, chopped

Sauté red onion until cooked through. Add prepared rice, cheese and eggs and combine.

Add pumpkin, pine nuts and spinach. Spoon mixture into muffin trays and bake in a preheated oven at 180°C for 15 - 20 minutes, or until cooked through and golden.

Suitable to freeze.

Nutrition information (per muffin): kilojoules 1040, calories 248, protein 12.5g, fat 15g, saturated fat 8g, carbohydrate 15g, fibre 1.5g.

If you are using our Nutrition for Weight Loss Surgery Meal Plans, one serve of this recipe provides the following number of serves from each of the following food groups:

1 GRAINS

1/2 PROTEIN

2 FATS

# Chicken, Bacon & Thyme Rice Muffins

MAKES 8 MUFFINS

1 red onion, finely diced
2/3 cup raw brown rice, prepared according to directions on packet
1 cup grated cheese
3 eggs, whisked
1 cooked chicken breast, shredded
3 rashers of lean bacon, cooked and diced
A few sprigs of thyme, chopped

Sauté red onion until cooked through. Add prepared rice, cheese and eggs and combine. Add shredded chicken, cooked bacon and thyme. Spoon mixture into muffin trays and bake in a pre-heated oven at 180°C for 15 - 20 minutes, or until cooked through and golden.

Suitable to freeze.

Nutrition information (per muffin): kilojoules 1150, calories 273, protein 21.5g, fat 15g, saturated fat 8.5g, carbohydrate 14.5g, fibre 1.5g.

If you are using our Nutrition for Weight Loss Surgery Meal Plans, one serve of this recipe provides the following number of serves from each of the following food groups:
1 GRAINS
1 PROTEIN
3 FATS

# Sweet Potato, Zucchini & Feta Mini Muffins

MAKES 30 MINI MUFFINS

1 medium sweet potato, grated
1 medium zucchini, grated
1 medium red onion, grated
½ cup grated cheese
100g feta, crumbled
1/3 cup spelt flour
4 eggs

Place all ingredients in a bowl and mix well. Spoon into greased mini muffin trays and bake in a preheated oven at 180°C for 15 minutes or until cooked through and golden.

Suitable to freeze.

Nutrition information (per 2 mini muffins): kilojoules 370, calories 89, protein 5.5g, fat 5.5g, saturated fat 3.5g, carbohydrate 4.5g, fibre 0.5g.

If you are using our Nutrition for Weight Loss Surgery Meal Plans, one serve of this recipe provides the following number of serves from each of the following food groups:
1 FATS
1/2 PROTEIN

# Bacon, Mushroom, Tomato & Egg Muffins

MAKES 6 MUFFINS

6 eggs
¼ cup milk
60g cheese, grated
2 rashers bacon, finely diced
3 button mushrooms, finely diced
1 tomato, finely diced

Whisk together eggs and milk, season to taste and set aside. Divide remaining ingredients between a six well muffin pan. Pour egg mixture over cheese, bacon, mushroom and tomato. Bake in a pre-heated oven at 180°C for 20 minutes, or until cooked through and golden.

Nutrition information (per muffin): kilojoules 575, calories 137, protein 12.5g, fat 9g, saturated fat 4.5g, carbohydrate 1.5g, fibre 0.5g.

If you are using our Nutrition for Weight Loss Surgery Meal Plans, one serve of this recipe provides the following number of serves from each of the following food groups:
1/2 PROTEIN
2 FATS

# Smoked Salmon, Cream Cheese & Dill Egg Muffins

MAKES 6 MUFFINS

6 eggs
¼ cup milk
60g cheese, grated
50g smoked salmon
6 teaspoons cream cheese
2 teaspoons chopped fresh dill

Whisk together eggs and milk, season to taste and set aside. Divide remaining ingredients between a six well muffin pan. Pour egg mixture over cheese, salmon, cream cheese and dill. Bake in a pre-heated oven at 180°C for 20 minutes, or until cooked through and golden.

Nutrition information (per muffin): kilojoules 527, calories 125, protein 10.5g, fat 9g, saturated fat 4.5g, carbohydrate 1g.

If you are using our Nutrition for Weight Loss Surgery Meal Plans, one serve of this recipe provides the following number of serves from each of the following food groups:
1/2 PROTEIN
2 FATS

# Chicken, Pesto & Pinenut Mini Meatloaves

MAKES 8 MINI MEATLOAVES

500g lean chicken mince
1 cup multigrain breadcrumbs
60g Parmesan cheese, grated
2 tablespoons basil pesto
1 tablespoon pine nuts, chopped
1 small red onion, grated
1 egg

Place ingredients in a bowl and mix well. Divide evenly into a muffin tray. Bake in a preheated oven at 180°C for 20 minutes or until cooked through and golden.

Suitable to freeze.

Nutrition information (per meatloaf): kilojoules 915, calories 218, protein 18g, fat 11.5g, saturated fat 3.5g, carbohydrate 11g, fibre 1g.

If you are using our Nutrition for Weight Loss Surgery Meal Plans, one serve of this recipe provides the following number of serves from each of the following food groups:
1 GRAINS
1 PROTEIN
2 FATS

# Italian Style Mini Meatloaves

MAKES 8 MINI MEATLOAVES

500g lean beef mince
1 cup multigrain breadcrumbs
2 eggs
1 clove garlic, crushed
1 brown onion, grated
1 small zucchini, grated and squeezed to remove excess water
1/3 cup sundried tomato pesto
½ cup Parmesan cheese, shredded
1 medium tomato, sliced

Combine all ingredients except tomato and Parmesan cheese in a bowl and mix well. Divide evenly into a muffin tray. Top with the Parmesan and sliced tomato. Bake in a preheated oven at 180°C for 20 minutes, or until cooked through and golden.

Suitable to freeze.

Nutritional information (per meatloaf): kilojoules 954, calories 237, protein 22.5g, fat 10g, saturated fat 4g, carbohydrate 13g, fibre 2g.

If you are using our Nutrition for Weight Loss Surgery Meal Plans, one serve of this recipe provides the following number of serves from each of the following food groups:
1 GRAINS
1 1/2 PROTEIN
2 FATS

# Turkey & Cranberry Mini Meatloaves

MAKES 8 MINI MEATLOAVES

500g lean turkey mince
1 cup multigrain breadcrumbs
1 egg
1 granny smith apple, grated
1 small brown onion, grated
2 tablespoons sage leaves, shredded
2 tablespoons dried cranberries
2 tablespoons cranberry sauce

Combine ingredients in a bowl reserving half of the cranberry sauce and mix well. Divide evenly into a muffin tray. Brush each mini meatloaf with the remaining cranberry sauce. Bake in a preheated oven at 180°C for 20 minutes or until cooked through and golden.

Suitable to freeze.

Nutrition information (per meatloaf): kilojoules 680, calories 162, protein 16.5g, fat 3g, saturated fat 1g, carbohydrate 17g, fibre 1.5g.

If you are using our Nutrition for Weight Loss Surgery Meal Plans, one serve of this recipe provides the following number of serves from each of the following food groups:
1 GRAINS
1 PROTEIN
1 FATS

# Pork, Apple & Pistachio Mini Meatloaves

MAKES 8 MINI MEATLOAVES

1 brown onion, grated
1 clove garlic, crushed
2 tablespoons fresh sage, chopped
500g lean pork mince
1 cup multigrain breadcrumbs
1 egg
½ cup apple puree
30g pistachio kernels

Sauté onion, garlic and sage. Combine remaining ingredients in a bowl, then add onion and garlic mixture and mix well. Divide evenly into a muffin tray. Bake in a preheated oven at 180°C for 20 minutes, or until cooked through and golden.

Suitable to freeze.

Nutrition information (per meatloaf): kilojoules 845, calories 201, protein 16.5g, fat 9g, saturated fat 2.5g, carbohydrate 13g, fibre 1.5g.

If you are using our Nutrition for Weight Loss Surgery Meal Plans, one serve of this recipe provides the following number of serves from each of the following food groups:
1 GRAINS
1 PROTEIN
2 FATS

# Enchilada Cups

MAKES 8 INDIVIDUAL ENCHILADA CUPS

1 onion, diced
Olive oil
500g lean chicken mince
Corn kernels, from 1 cob of corn
425g tin of black beans, drained
1 jar enchilada sauce
8 mini corn tortillas
80g cheese, grated
Avocado, diced tomato, jalapeños and
Greek yoghurt, to serve

Sauté onion until cooked in a drizzle of olive oil. Add chicken mince and brown. Add corn, black beans and enchilada sauce and mix through. Place corn tortillas into a muffin tray and top with chicken mixture. Sprinkle with cheese and bake in a preheated oven for 15 minutes at 180°C, or until cooked through. Remove from muffin tray and top with diced avocado, tomato, jalapeños and Greek yoghurt.

Nutrition information (per enchilada cup): kilojoules 980, calories 233, protein 20g, fat 9.5g, saturated fat 4g, carbohydrate 14.5g, fibre 6g.

If you are using our Nutrition for Weight Loss Surgery Meal Plans, one serve of this recipe provides the following number of serves from each of the following food groups:
1 GRAINS
1 PROTEIN
2 FATS

# Lasagne Muffins

MAKES 6 LASAGNE MUFFINS

12 wonton wrappers
60g ricotta
1 cup (¼ recipe) meat sauce (page 29)
30g parmesan
50g cheese, grated

Layer wonton wrappers, ricotta, meat sauce, Parmesan and grated cheese into muffin trays then repeat so you have two layers (2 wonton wrappers per muffin). Bake in a preheated oven at 180°C for 20 minutes or until cooked through and golden.

Suitable to freeze.

Nutrition information (per muffin): kilojoules 710, calories 170g, protein 12.5g, fat 8g, saturated fat 4.5g, carbohydrate 12g, fibre 0.5g.

If you are using our Nutrition for Weight Loss Surgery Meal Plans, one serve of this recipe provides the following number of serves from each of the following food groups:
1 GRAINS
1/2 PROTEIN
2 FATS

# Ramekins

............................

*Ramekins are a super simple way to serve the right amount of your favourite family meals and comfort foods following surgery and are great to freeze meals in single serves.*

*Keep a collection of bright and interesting ramekins on hand to help make slow cooked dishes, curries, casseroles, mornays and stews look like they have come straight from your favourite cafe.*

# Mini Shepard's Pie

MAKES 6 SMALL RAMEKINS

2 cups (½ recipe) meat sauce (page 29)
¼ large cauliflower
40g ricotta
40g cheese, grated
Smoked paprika

Divide meat sauce evenly between six ramekins. Steam cauliflower until tender, then mash together with ricotta. Season to taste. Top mince mixture with cauliflower mash, grated cheese and smoked paprika. Bake in a preheated oven at 180°C for 20 minutes, or until golden.

Suitable to freeze.

Nutritional information (per ramekin): kilojoules 945, calories 225, protein 22g, fat 12g, saturated fat 5.5g, carbohydrate 5.5g, fibre 3g.

If you are using our Nutrition for Weight Loss Surgery Meal Plans, one serve of this recipe provides the following number of serves from each of the following food groups:
1 PROTEIN
2 FATS
1/2 GRAINS

# Basic Meat Sauce

MAKES 4 CUPS OR 8 X 1/2 CUP SERVES

1 medium brown onion, finely diced
2 stalks celery, finely diced
1 medium carrot, finely diced or grated
2 garlic cloves, crushed
4 mushrooms, finely diced
2 tablespoons tomato paste
1 tablespoon olive oil
500g lean beef mince
400g tin tomatoes, diced
2 tablespoon Worcestershire sauce
2 teaspoons dried oregano
Salt and pepper to taste

Sauté onion, celery, carrot, garlic and mushrooms in olive oil until tender, add mince and tomato paste and brown. Add tomatoes, Worcestershire and oregano, bring to a simmer and cook for 20 minutes.

This sauce can be used in the Shepherd's Pie and Lasagna Muffin recipes, or:

- Top baked potatoes/sweet potatoes or grainy toast
- Serve with zoodles/pasta/cauliflower rice or steamed vegetables
- Fill tacos
- Keep one cup portions in the freezer for quick, easy meals.

Nutritional information (per half cup serve): kilojoules 670, calories 160, protein 17.5g, fat 7.5g, saturated fat 2.5g, carbohydrate 4g, fibre 1.5g.

If you are using our Nutrition for Weight Loss Surgery Meal Plans, one serve of this recipe provides the following number of serves from each of the following food groups:
1 PROTEIN
2 FATS

# Mini Mexican Chicken Bowls

MAKES 6 MINI BOWLS

500g skinless chicken, diced (thigh or tenderloin work well)
1 red onion, sliced
300g jar of salsa
400g can four or five bean mix, drained
Corn, avocado, tomato and coriander to serve

Place chicken, onion, salsa and bean mix in a slow cooker on high for four hours. When cooked, divide between 6 small ramekins. Top with a salad of corn, avocado, tomato and coriander just before serving.

Suitable to freeze (without salad).

Nutritional information (without salad): kilojoules 730, calories 175, protein 24g, fat 1.5g, saturated fat 0.5g, carbohydrate 13g, fibre 5g.

If you are using our Nutrition for Weight Loss Surgery Meal Plans, one serve of this recipe provides the following number of serves from each of the following food groups:
1 GRAINS
1 1/2 PROTEIN

# Chicken Curry with Pappadums

MAKES 4 ONE CUP CURRIES

500g skinless chicken, diced (thigh or tenderloin work well)
1 small sweet potato, diced
¼ cup red lentils
400ml passata (tomato puree)
1 red onion, sliced
1 garlic clove, crushed
1.5cm piece of ginger, grated
½ teaspoon ground cardamom
1 teaspoon garam masala
1 teaspoon ground coriander
¼ teaspoon chili powder (or to taste)
4 pappadums (one per serve)

Add all ingredients, except pappadums, to slow cooker and cook on low for six hours. Once cooked, spoon one cup of curry into each ramekin and top with one crushed pappadum. Sprinkle with coriander to serve.

Suitable to freeze (without pappadums).

Nutritional information: kilojoules 695, calories 165, protein 29.5g, fat 2.3g, saturated fat 0.5g, carbohydrate 6g, fibre 1g.

If you are using our Nutrition for Weight Loss Surgery Meal Plans, one serve of this recipe provides the following number of serves from each of the following food groups:
1/2 GRAINS
1 1/2 PROTEIN
1/2 FATS

# Salmon Mornay

MAKES 6 INDIVIDUAL MORNAYS

400g salmon, diced
2 cups milk
2 tablespoons margarine or butter
2 tablespoons flour
4 medium eggs, hard-boiled, chopped
2 teaspoons capers
1 gherkin, diced
Juice of half a lemon
Cracked pepper, to taste
4 tablespoons wholegrain breadcrumbs
Smoked paprika

Place diced salmon and milk in a saucepan and simmer. Remove fish from milk and set the milk aside. Divide fish between 6 ramekins. Place butter and flour in a saucepan and cook off to form a roux, slowly pour in the poaching milk and stir until sauce thickens. Divide eggs, capers and gherkins between ramekins, squeeze over fresh lemon and cracked pepper. Pour over white sauce and sprinkle with breadcrumbs and smoked paprika. Bake in a preheated oven for 15 minutes at 180°C, or until golden.

Suitable to freeze.

Nutritional information: kilojoules 1250, calories 297, protein 26.5g, fat 15.5g, saturated fat 4.5g, carbohydrate 12.5g, fibre 0.5g.

If you are using our Nutrition for Weight Loss Surgery Meal Plans, one serve of this recipe provides the following number of serves from each of the following food groups:
1 GRAINS
1 1/2 PROTEIN
3 FATS

# Chicken, Leak & Mushroom Pie

MAKES 6 INDIVIDUAL PIES

500g skinless chicken, diced (thigh or tenderloin work well)
2 tablespoons flour
Olive oil
1 leek, cut in half lengthways, finely sliced
50g bacon, diced
150g mushrooms, diced
1/3 cup white wine (optional)
1 cup chicken stock
2 teaspoons Dijon mustard
1 teaspoon dried mixed herbs
½ cup light sour cream
2 slices wholegrain toast, cubed

Place chicken and flour in a zip lock bag and shake to coat. Sauté leek, bacon and mushrooms in a little olive oil. Once tender, add chicken and an extra drizzle of oil and cook until browned. Add wine, chicken stock, mustard and herbs. Bring to a simmer and cook for 5 minutes. Remove from heat and stir through sour cream. Spoon chicken mixture into ramekins and top with cubed bread. Bake in a pre-heated oven for 15 minutes at 180°C.

Suitable to freeze (without bread).

Nutritional information (without bread): kilojoules 855, calories 203, protein 25g, fat 6g, saturated fat 2.6g, carbohydrate 10g, fibre 0.5g.

If you are using our Nutrition for Weight Loss Surgery Meal Plans, one serve of this recipe provides the following number of serves from each of the following food groups:
1/2 GRAINS
1 1/2 PROTEIN
1 FATS

All rights reserved. No part of this publication may be reproduced, stored in a retrieval system or transmitted in any form or by any means, electronic, mechanical, photocopying, recording or otherwise, without the prior written permission of the author.

The moral rights of the author have been asserted.

Copyright © Nutrition for Weight Loss Surgery 2018

Recipe Development: Justine Hawke
Food Styling and Photography: Alexandra Gow
Edited by Justine Hawke and Sally Johnston.

www.nfwls.com

www.ingramcontent.com/pod-product-compliance
Lightning Source LLC
Chambersburg PA
CBHW061817290426
44110CB00026B/2894